Twelve Bars and the Truth

P.J. Lenox

BookLeaf Publishing

Presentation by *BookLeaf Publishing*

Web: www.bookleafpub.com

E-mail: info@bookleafpub.com

ISBN: 978-93-5744-712-6

First edition 2021

Dedicated specially to Melody, Al, Brenda, and
Patrick for unconditional support.

ACKNOWLEDGEMENT

Grateful acknowledgement to Memory Rose,
wherever she is, nobody knows.

PREFACE

These poems are meant to be read out loud. They describe feelings, a state of mind, but mostly, struggling through life long enough to sing about it.

Twelve bars and the truth,
When it hurts you too,
That's the blues.

- P.J. Lenox

Insomnia

It's two A.M.,
Can't sleep,
Insomnia on a Tuesday.
I hear the clock,
Tick, tick, tick,
Got the blues in a few ways.
It's a long night,
No shut eye,
Can't turn my mind off.
Thoughts come in,
Think, think, think,
Evaporate like rain drops.

Can't breathe,
Breathe,
Breathe.

Spent all day
Working hard,
Trying to earn a quick buck.
My feet are tired,
Run, run, run,
Can't stop and get stuck.
I feel down,
Feel like shit,
Feel like I'm doing things wrong.

All day,
Lie, lie, lie,
Can't keep up for that long.

Can't breathe,
Breathe,
Breathe.

Expectations,
What's the point?
Be a man and hold up.
Like my pop,
Work, work, work,
Put it all on the young pups.
They say to me,
"You're on track!"
Like I have a success kit.
My ma' says "keep,"
Keep, keep, keep,
Keep going and I'll make it.

Just breathe,
Breathe,
Breathe.

Fuck the plans,
I breathe chaos,
I'm like a blackbird singing.
My mind goes on,

And on, and on,
But I like the sound of the ringing.
My hands burn,
My head aches,
My heart's out of my chest.
I finally feel,
Feel, feel, feel,
This bird's left the nest.

Sing,
Sing,
Sing!

It's three A.M.,
Can't sleep,
Insomnia on a Tuesday.
I hear the clock,
Tick, tick, tick,
I'm hopeful in a few ways.
It's a long night,
No shut eye,
Don't want to turn my mind off,
Emotions spread,
Feel so good,
Form puddles out of raindrops.

Tell Me Mama

Tell me mama, what's in your eyes?
I see glowing green fireflies,
When you cry, I'll collect your tears,
Water the roses,
And bring them to you, my dear.

Tell me mama, why are you so sweet?
I taste your honey and buzz like a bee,
When I'm thirsty, you get me drunk,
I float in your glass,
Even when I feel sunk.

Tell me mama, what's in your heart?
I see finches fly in pairs, not apart,
When you're hurting, I'll sing you rhymes,
Mend your wings,
It'll just take a little time.

Tell me mama, what's in your smile?
When I'm tired and I hiked for miles,
The sun blinds me, you always know,
I need your beaming,
To ease my weary soul.

How can you stay so still?

How can you stay so still?
For when rabbits stop running,
Bald eagles sweep over the hills,
The rabbit is quick, but the eagle is patient and
cunning.

How can you stay so still?
For the river floods the land,
The desert turns the sky sterile,
The river is strong, but the desert roughly
withstands.

How can you stay so still?
For when trees stop growing,
The logger sends it to the mill,
The tree was older, but the mill is uncaring and
unknowing.

How can you stay so still?
For when caterpillars cocoon,
Daughters of the sun emerge with will,
Butterflies rise high, no cage can confine them
in the midst of June.

How can you stay so still?

It's as miserable outside as I am

It's as miserable outside as I am,
The sky is grey with grief,
The clouds are dark with disparity,
I think they will weep.

It's as lonely outside as I am,
The ocean's blue and bleak,
The waves are small and sympathetic,
I think I will sink.

As a Bumblebee flies on to a Sunflower

As a bumblebee flies on to a sunflower,
He is quickly intoxicated by her scent,
And if he only lived another hour,
That hour would be the most joyful existence.

When it rains, sometimes it pours

When the sun comes up I'm thinking,
What's the point of going on?
I pay my bills, do my job,
But the struggle is just too hard.

Why does every morning feel like a mourn?
Mama always says when it rains, sometimes it
pours.

Some days I try my best,
To be happy with who I am.
I look at other people,
And I want to be happy like them.

Maybe I'm just starting to get a little bit too
bored.
My mama always says when it rains, sometimes
it pours.

I walk around feeling like
My legs are made of bricks.
My brain is full of thoughts,
But my mind says, "Go back to bed."

I swear I feel like I'm one-hundred and four.

*But mama always says when it rains, sometimes
it pours.*

At night I lie awake, thinking
And looking at my wife.
She deserves someone better,
Who says things that are nice.

*I think it would be best if I walked right out the
door.
Mama always said when it rains, sometimes it
pours.*

Spitting out salt and wading through waves

Playing piano and praying for rain,
I sat pounding the keys and searching in vain,
Going from G sharp to B flat to C to F,
Listening to missed notes until I go deaf.

But my fingers stopped, before my heart stopped,
And suddenly, silence.

Sifting through sonnets and looking for lines,
Words to inspire and inflame my romantic mind,
Recalling the chapter, the poem, the verse, the
letter,
Bitter love makes life feel better.

But my eyes blurred, before my mind blurred,
And suddenly, darkness.

Spitting out salt and wading through waves,
The ocean's my queen and I am her knave,
I looked down and saw mixture of water, rocks,
blood, and sand,
I feel so alive with all four staining my hand.

My skin stirs, then my soul stirs,
And suddenly, I'm reborn.

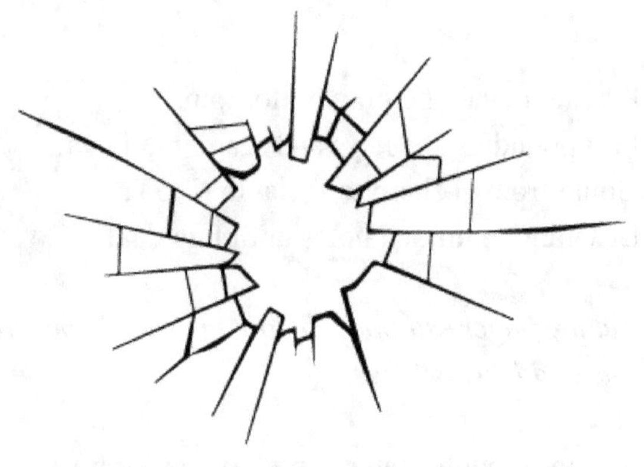

Snow Fell Like Mortal Fragments

The sky was dull and grey,
With blue around the edges,
And somewhere out there beyond,
Snow fell like mortal fragments.

Curious I stumbled,
To where the lake had frozen,
I stepped onto the ice,
The lake hissed and crackled.

Standing in leather boots,
I bent down to tighten the laces,
Suddenly I realized,
I could hear the fish speaking.

I took off my coat and shoes,
So I could hear them better,
They swam laughing, playing,
A natural, deep connection.

Reaching into my coat,
I took a wooden locket,
The lake beneath me listened,
And she melted open a spot.

I plunged my hand inside,

The water numbed all sensation,
But I felt my hand open,
Releasing my soul with it.

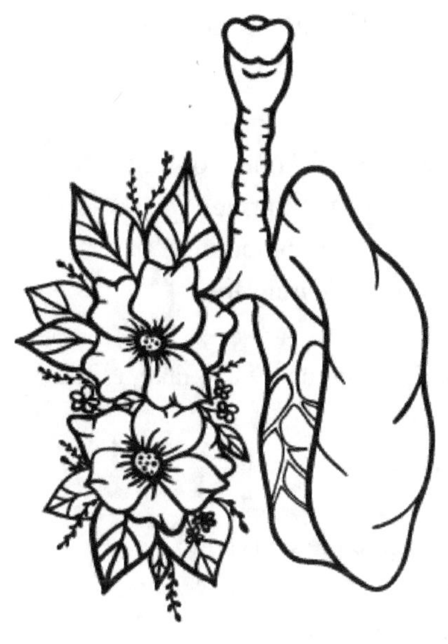

Paradise Lost Blues

Adam was cruisin' one morning,
In the heart of the Spring,
The flowers were blooming,
And Eve was floating free.

She said, "Maybe you can take a little
Drive with me,
Your nature can be mine.

Eve said give me your hand,
Gentle as you may,
Feel my skin softly,
It's enough to make you pray.

She said, "Maybe you can take a little
Drive with me,
Your nature can be mine."

She showed him a rose,
Put it in a rope,
He gave it a tug,
Then the stem broke.

She said, "Maybe you can take a little
Drive with me,
Your nature can be mine."

Adam turned to her,
Told her knowledge is king,
When Paradise is lost,
We can rewrite everything.

He said, "Maybe you can take a little
Drive with me,
Your nature can be mine.

Bear to bare,
Bee to be,
Never mind our nature,
You can buy yourself free.

He said, "Maybe you can take a little
Drive with me,
Your nature can be mine."

He pulled Eve's ear and whispered,
"What's the cost of your mind?"
He took a bite of snake,
Told her it's sweet as apple pie.

He said, "Maybe you can take a little
Drive with me,
Your nature can be mine."

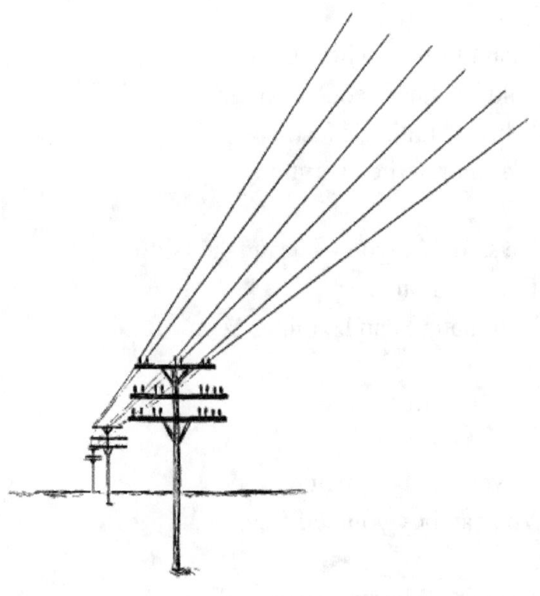

Move On Blues

I wake up on the weekend,
At my window, birds chirping,
My phone starts to buzz,
Telling me what celebs are tweeting.
Someone's flashing Chanel,
Someone else is flashing Coach,
Out the window there's a bluebird,
Picking up a fresh worm.

> With the sunrise,
> Lighting up the black sky,
> We both move on.

A privileged kid goes flying by,
While I'm walking past the highway,
Passing up a homeless man,
Looking for a little change.
Kid thinks he's got the nice rims,
Thinks he's got a nice ride,
Thinking the homeless man is drinking,
But he's only drinking gasoline.

> With the sunset,
> Coloring the dark sky,
> They both move on.

I'm swinging by a nightclub,
The beat is blaring outside,
People passing kilos,
I hop to a bar with keys inside.
The pianist is pouring,
His fingers are bleeding,
His fingers speak for his soul,
But I'm the only one listening.

> With the moonlight,
> Shining in the night sky,
> We both move on.

On my way back home,
Swimming through a sea of screens,
People hoping for a hook-up,
Eyes blinded but still searching.
They're looking for a quick lay,
Swiping every direction,
I guess that we are all just,
Looking for a connection.

> With the sunrise,
> Lighting up the black sky,
> We all move on.

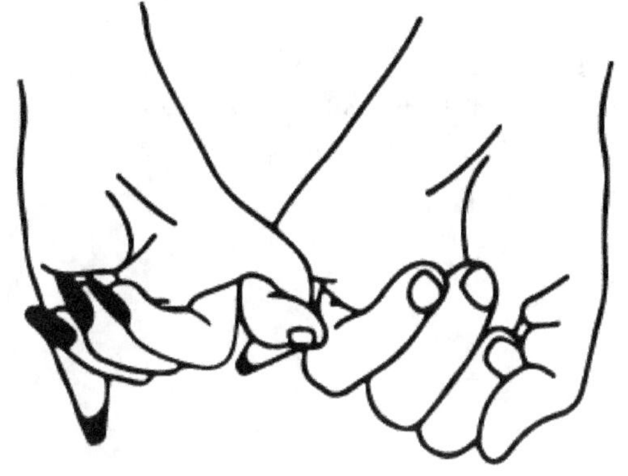

a Rose without a thorn

she said my dear don't worry,
the sun will rise and keep you warm,
and when it does, I'll pick you,
a Rose without a thorn.

A Nightly Proposal

30

Joy and pure elation shone from the full moon to
the bay,
As he sang so soft and sweetly in the air of early
May,
Through the fog, illumination as he held his
hand to the horizon,
He wept crying, crashing waves as he proposed
she be his one.

A Tempest

I have learned that the simplest thing
Is to sit in the sun and watch the sea,
While the wind stirs the waves swiftly
Toward the shore.

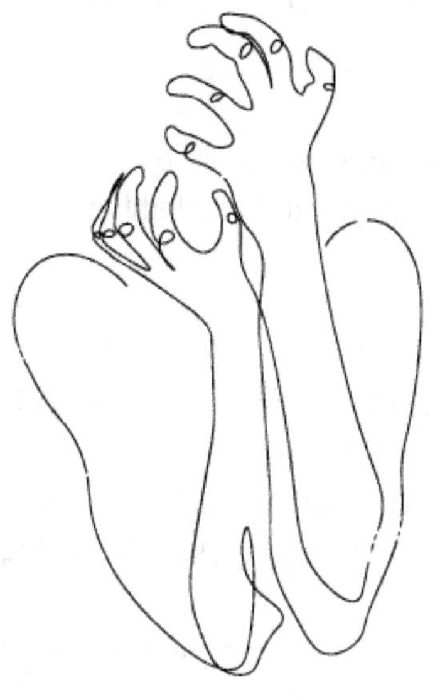

Mortality, Myth, and Sin

Picture this in your mind's eye,
Take humanity, put it in a bubble.

Silence.

Then an explosion of sound, you can hear the
colors,
What did God feel like as the creator?
And what of the ringing sound echoing in the
stars?
One day to be drowned out by the sound of car
horns and car alarms.
He couldn't have known one day,
Morality would affect mortality,
And rivers of blood would flood the streets,
Like red wine staining your blankets, pillows,
and sheets.

Mortality.

That prostitution would be common,
So that a single mother wouldn't starve her son,
And that you'd trust her more than you trust the
police,
Because you don't want to wind up dead or
beaten.

That a pastor would steal from the poor,
And he ain't no better than a dime store robber,
Who stole a couple of cans and maybe some
milk,
To take to his family because he had to pay a
mortgage bill.

Myth.

Is it enough that the people you trust would rob
you and let you die,
While politicians would prefer that you stay
blind?
And that all the indifference and loudest
opinions,
Would drive us apart like a creek turning into a
river.
It's enough to make you reconsider your
religion,
The devil preys upon your moral weakness,
He has poems to sell your soul for and he could
drown out the sound,
And he'd wrap it in a bubble and blow it all up.

Sin.

Until you're left with an explosion,
And a dizzying feeling,
You question your existence,

And whether or not you are present or missing.
You no longer wonder what it would be like to
play God,
Because your ears ring loud like church bells,
Your skin burns hot as hell but feels cold as sin,
And the stars sing like mythical fragments to
your mortal ears.

Sound.

So you start to think about reality,
The explosion was real, but where did it lead?
The answers are real, but they leave you reeling,
Because you have feelings and emotions you are
still living.
So if you are out there,
Answer me if you can,
What is the price of humanity,
Is it mortality, myth, or sin?

Picture this in your mind's eye,
Take humanity, put it in a bubble.

Pop.

God. Guns. and Gold.

God and guns, guns and gold,
White bread, white fences,
Segregated neighborhoods.
God and guns, guns and gold,
White skin, white collar,
Who runs the schools?

Your kids are on the corner,
Staring at an ice cream truck,
Picking their favorite flavors,
No vanilla, out of luck.
My kids are on the border,
Staring at a wall,
Being called criminals,
Before they can even crawl.

God and guns, guns and gold,
White faith, white rights,
Wonder who's in control?
God and guns, guns and gold,
White race, white pride,
What a wonderful world.

You got a good job,
CEO nine to five,
You pass us on the overpass,

But don't bat an eye.
You say we took your jobs,
We're in the fields five to nine,
Picking all your fruit,
You want I.C.E. but also wine.

God and guns, guns and gold,
White house, white privilege,
Euro history books.
God and guns, guns and gold,
White walls, white lines,
Why is life so good?

You said all we do,
Is bring crime and rape,
Nobody asked the wetback,
About walls, war, or dates.
You said all we are,
Is low-life deadbeats,
We work for a couple bucks,
While your business steals like thieves.

We're not the ones who raped the land,
We didn't steal from "Indians,"
We're not proud to be "Americans,"
We're not the ones who want,
God. Guns. and Gold.

Super Glue, a Snack, and more Sleep

I've been slipping up, falling down, running
around in circles,
Chasing my tail, like a dog,
Too impatient to hunt a squirrel.
I've been rising up, tumbling, and dusting off my
jacket,
I'm like a hotel with a penthouse,
And a basement without an exit.

Folktales taught me every princess has a prince,
And you should hold them tight so they don't slip
out of your hands,
But I have a question, I don't want contrivance
or suggestions,
Did Snow White really just want to sleep for one
more day?

I can't sleep, but I can't stay awake,
My life has been crumbling like soft soil after
rain.
My worries have been blooming like a garden of
weeds,
I think I need a super glue, a snack, and more
sleep.

I've been burning quick, like a matchstick,
flickering toward my fingertips,
I never talk, but when I do,
I say some stupid, shameful shit.
I don't want to get up, don't want to stop, don't
want to open my eyes,
The night's just long and dark enough,
To design a dream and fantasize.

*Folktales taught me every villain has an evil
plan,*
*But they hold them so tightly that the pain will
make them wince,*
*And I have a question, I don't want contrivance
or suggestions,*
*Was Sleeping Beauty resting really such an
awful fate?*

I can't sleep, but I can't stay awake,
My life has been crumbling, like soft soil after
rain.
My worries have been blooming like a garden of
weeds,
I think I need super glue, a snack, and more
sleep.

Flowers (Springtime Blues)

Flowers exploded like fireworks,
And the dark soil was suddenly light.
The bees wrote the soundtrack,
Their harmony buzzed and rhymed.
But Mother Nature reconsidered,
And raindrops fell from my eyes.

Ninety-Nine Degrees (River Basin Blues)

Ain't got no money,
Ain't got no car,
My baby left me for temptation.
It's ninety-nine degrees outside,
And there ain't no water in the river basin.

She lied to me,
She did not tell the truth,
I guess she's got an active imagination.
It's ninety-nine degrees outside,
And there ain't no water in the river basin.

Ain't got no baby,
Ain't got no honey,
I don't got no romantic relations.
It's ninety-nine degrees outside,
And there ain't no water in the river basin.

I think I'll move on,
And live on the Colorado,
I'll pack it up if I find the inspiration.
It's ninety-nine degrees outside,
And I can't drown in the river basin.

No Coat (The Fall Blues)

The seasons are changin',
A cold wind's startin' to blow,
And my baby wrote me a letter,
She said, "I took yo' heavy coat."

Snow (Cold Winter Blues)

I had the blues fall down, and melt in the palm
of my hand,
      Palm of my hand.
It was cold and wet, like ocean water on the
sand,
      On the sand.
I said the blues are beautiful,
But they sting me so bad.

I held a needle in my hand, stitched my arm with
a quick sew,
      With a quick sew.
I held up my arm and saw more blood drip
below,
      Drip below.
I looked outside and wondered,
How cold was that snow?

I Heard One-Thousand Drums
Pounding

I heard one-thousand drums,
Pounding,
Pounding,
Pounding in my head.

Water falling on the sidewalk,
Dripping,
Dripping,
Dripping in an abrupt beat.

My thoughts whispered,
Hush,
Hush,
And tortured my ears deaf.